Date: 11/25/13

J 796.33263 HOW
Howell, Brian,
Miami Hurricanes /

PALM BEACH COUNTY
LIBRARY SYSTEM
3650 SUMMIT BLVD.
WEST PALM BEACH, FL 33406

MIAMI HURRICANES

BY BRIAN HOWELL

Published by ABDO Publishing Company, PO Box 398166, Minneapolis, MN 55439. Copyright © 2013 by Abdo Consulting Group, Inc. International copyrights reserved in all countries. No part of this book may be reproduced in any form without written permission from the publisher. SportsZone™ is a trademark and logo of ABDO Publishing Company.

Printed in the United States of America,
North Mankato, Minnesota
102012
012013

 THIS BOOK CONTAINS AT LEAST 10% RECYCLED MATERIALS.

Editor: Chrös McDougall
Series Designer: Craig Hinton

Photo Credits: Cover, Joe Sebo/AP Images, 1; Paul Sakuma/AP Images, 4, 9, 43 (bottom); Dean Hoffmeyer/Richmond Times-Dispatch/AP Images, 7; Marta Lavandier/AP Images, 11, 37; Mark J. Terrill/AP Images, 12; John Van Beekum/Miami Herald/AP Images, 14; AP Images, 19, 25, 42 (top), 43 (top right); Ted Powers/AP Images, 20, 43 (top left); John Raoux/AP Images, 23; Raul Demolina/AP Images, 27, 42 (bottom left); Tannen Maury/AP Images, 28; Al Messerschmidt/Getty Images, 31, 42 (bottom right); Jeffrey Boan/AP Images, 33; Eric Draper/AP Images, 34; Luis M. Alvarez/AP Images, 39; Cal Sport Media via AP Images, 41; Hans Heryk/AP Images, 44

Library of Congress Cataloging-in-Publication Data
Howell, Brian.
 Miami Hurricanes / Brian Howell.
  p. cm. -- (Inside college football)
Includes bibliographical references and index.
ISBN 978-1-61783-654-1
1. Miami Hurricanes (Football team)--History--Juvenile literature. 2. University of Miami--Football--History--Juvenile literature. I. Title.
796.332--dc15

2012945711

TABLE OF CONTENTS

1. HURRICANES DOMINATE THE COUNTRY 5
2. SETTING THE FOUNDATION ... 15
3. HURRICANES REACH THE TOP 21
4. TRADITION CONTINUES 29
5. SEEKING A RETURN TO THE TOP 35

TIMELINE 42

QUICK STATS 44

QUOTES & ANECDOTES 45

GLOSSARY 46

FOR MORE INFORMATION 47

INDEX 48

ABOUT THE AUTHOR 48

Miami's Andre Johnson, *left*, and Jeremy Shockey celebrate after Johnson scored a touchdown in the 2002 Rose Bowl.

HURRICANES DOMINATE THE COUNTRY

MIAMI HURRICANES JUNIOR QUARTERBACK KEN DORSEY DROPPED BACK TO PASS. SOPHOMORE WIDE RECEIVER ANDRE JOHNSON WAS SPRINTING ALL ALONE DOWN THE FIELD, SO DORSEY LET THE BALL FLY. IT LANDED PERFECTLY IN JOHNSON'S ARMS. HE THEN CARRIED IT INTO THE END ZONE FOR A 49-YARD TOUCHDOWN. JUST LIKE THAT, THE HURRICANES WERE OFF AND RUNNING.

On the night of January 3, 2002, the University of Miami football team routed the Nebraska Cornhuskers 37–14 in the Rose Bowl. The win finished off a remarkable season for the Hurricanes. They went 12–0 and rolled through almost every team they played. Many considered the 2001 Hurricanes to be one of the most dominant teams in college football history. The Rose Bowl victory sealed the school's fifth consensus national championship, and its first in 10 years.

"It feels better than I thought it would," said star junior running back Clinton Portis.

HURRICANES

PURE WINNER

Despite his lean, 6-foot-5, 200-pound frame, Ken Dorsey put together one of the finest careers of any Miami quarterback. In three years as a starter, he led the Hurricanes to a 38–2 record. Through 2011, no Hurricanes quarterback had won more games. Along the way, Dorsey broke numerous school records, including total offense (9,486 yards), career passing yards (9,565), and career touchdown passes (86). He also threw a touchdown pass in 31 straight games.

In 2001, Dorsey finished third in voting for the Heisman Trophy. It is given to the best college football player each season. He won the Maxwell Award that year, though. It is a separate player-of-the-year award. He also was a Heisman finalist in 2002. After college, Dorsey spent six years as a backup in the National Football League (NFL).

Since the early 1980s, Miami had been one of the best college football teams in the country. The Hurricanes had won five national titles and been in the hunt for others. They had also built a reputation for being arrogant. But they backed it up on the field. As good as the Hurricanes had been through the years, the 2001 team might have been the best in school history.

The foundation for 2001 was set a year earlier. In 2000, the Hurricanes lost 34–29 at Washington in their second game of the season. They went 10–0 the rest of the way, though. Miami finished ranked second in the country. Many believed the Hurricanes should have played in the Orange Bowl that year. It served as that season's Bowl Championship Series (BCS) national championship game. The BCS determines the best teams in the country using a system of polls and other data and then places those teams in BCS bowls.

Quarterback Ken Dorsey led the Hurricanes to 38 wins during his three years as the starter from 2000 to 2002.

Miami instead went to the Sugar Bowl, another BCS bowl, and beat Florida 37–20. Florida State, which lost to Miami that season, went to the Orange Bowl and lost 13–2 to Oklahoma.

Miami coach Butch Davis left the school to take a head coaching job with the NFL's Cleveland Browns after that season. But new coach

Larry Coker kept the winning going. It helped that the Hurricanes were loaded with talent.

Dorsey was one of the best quarterbacks in the country. And Portis was one of the country's finest running backs. Johnson and junior tight end Jeremy Shockey were among the best at their positions, too. The offensive line had two All-American tackles, seniors Joaquin Gonzalez and Bryant McKinnie. All of them eventually went on to the NFL. Two other offensive line players—junior center Brett Romberg and senior guard Martin Bibla—also went on to play in the NFL.

Defensively, the Hurricanes might have been even better. Of the 11 starters, eight went on to become first-round picks in the NFL Draft. And 10 of the starters played at least one year in the NFL.

All-American senior safety Ed Reed led the way. But cornerbacks senior Mike Rumph and junior Phillip Buchanon were stars, too. Reed, Rumph, and Buchanon were first-round NFL Draft picks in 2002. Junior defensive linemen William Joseph and Jerome McDougle were

ALL-AMERICANS

Miami had six first-team All-Americans in 2001. They were Phillip Buchanon (punt returner), Joaquin Gonzalez (right tackle), Bryant McKinnie (left tackle), Ed Reed (safety), Jeremy Shockey (tight end), and Todd Sievers (kicker). In addition, the Associated Press (AP) named quarterback Ken Dorsey a second-team All-American. Running back Clinton Portis, offensive lineman Martin Bibla, and defensive linemen William Joseph and Jerome McDougle made the AP third team.

Miami quarterback Ken Dorsey hands the ball off to running back Clinton Portis in the 2002 Rose Bowl.

first-round picks in 2003. And sophomore linebackers Jonathan Vilma and D. J. Williams, and freshman safety Sean Taylor, were first-round picks in 2004.

"We talk about talent all along, but the thing that set this team apart is character," Coker said. "They refused to give in, refused to flinch, and they got the job done week in and week out."

Miami opened the 2001 season with a 33–7 rout of Penn State. Then it crushed Rutgers 61–0. The Hurricanes were not truly tested

HURRICANES

until their eighth game, against the Boston College Eagles. That game featured one of the most memorable plays in team history. Miami held a slim 12–7 lead in the final minutes of the game. But Boston College had a first down at Miami's 9-yard line. Eagles quarterback Brian St. Pierre threw a pass that hit off of Rumph's knee and bounced into the arms of Miami junior lineman Matt Walters. Walters started running. The Boston College players began to tackle him. But before Walters went down, Reed took the ball out of Walters's hands. Reed then dodged Eagles defenders on the way to a 91-yard touchdown that sealed an 18–9 win.

The next week, Miami pounded fourteenth-ranked Syracuse 59–0. The Hurricanes crushed twelfth-ranked Washington 65–7 the week after that. No team had ever defeated back-to-back ranked teams in such dominating fashion.

All that stood in the way of the Hurricanes' path to the national title game was a visit to fourteenth-ranked Virginia Tech. That game on December 1 started out like so many other Miami games. Dorsey threw

HIGH CHARACTER

During Miami's dominance of the 1980s and 1990s, the Hurricanes were known as much for their trash-talking and off-the-field troubles as they were for their winning. The 2001 Hurricanes prided themselves on the fact that they had players who stayed out of trouble and did not get involved in trash talking. "We have a lot of quiet, easygoing guys like me, who leave it all on the field," sophomore linebacker Jonathan Vilma said. "People talk at us, and we listen and say, 'That's nice. Now look at the scoreboard.'"

Miami tight end Jeremy Shockey stretches for a touchdown during a 2001 game against West Virginia.

a touchdown pass to Shockey. Portis ran for another touchdown. Miami held a 20–3 lead at halftime. The lead stretched to 26–10 in the fourth quarter. Virginia Tech roared back to bring the score to 26–24. But Miami was able to hold on and finish off a perfect regular season.

There was no doubt top-ranked Miami belonged in the Rose Bowl—that year's national championship game. There was plenty of debate about the Hurricanes' opponent, however. Colorado, Florida, Nebraska, and Oregon all believed they deserved a crack at the Hurricanes in the title game. In the end, it was Nebraska that got the opportunity to face the Hurricanes. Some would say it was a misfortune.

"If you have any more questions, we're 12–0," Reed said after beating Nebraska for the national title. "There's a lot of people saying

Miami wide receiver Andre Johnson kisses the national championship trophy after the 2002 Rose Bowl.

they should be here [in Nebraska's spot]. If they were, they would have gotten the same treatment."

Miami outscored its opponents 512–117 that season. It won by an average of 32.9 points per game—still the largest average margin in Miami history through 2011. The 512 points were the most in school history to that point. The 2002 Hurricanes later broke that record with 527 points, although that came in 13 games. The 2001 defense also was strong. It led the country in several major categories and even scored eight touchdowns.

Miami flashed all of its weapons against Nebraska. Dorsey threw for 362 yards, and Johnson caught seven passes for 199 yards. They were named the game's co-Most Valuable Players. The defense shut down Nebraska quarterback Eric Crouch, who won the Heisman Trophy that season.

In the end, it was a classic Miami performance that again put the Hurricanes at the top of the college football world. And Miami nearly won another title the next season. The Hurricanes started the 2002 season 12–0, stretching their win streak to 34. But a double-overtime loss to Ohio State in the Fiesta Bowl ended that. While disappointments in 2000 and 2002 prevented Miami from winning three championships in a row, Hurricanes fans are not likely to forget the greatness of the 2001 team.

AWARD WINNERS

Miami had several players win national awards in the years surrounding the 2001 national championship. Tackle Bryant McKinnie was the 2001 winner of the Outland Trophy, which is given to the nation's top lineman. Linebacker Dan Morgan won the 2000 Bednarik Award and Nagurski Trophy, which are separate awards given to the top defensive players in the country. He also won the Butkus Award, which is given to the country's top linebacker. Morgan was Miami's all-time leading tackler through 2011. Center Brett Romberg won the 2002 Rimington Trophy, which is given to the nation's best center. And in 2003, tight end Kellen Winslow Jr. became Miami's only winner of the Mackey Award, which is given to the nation's best tight end.

The University of Miami opened in 1925. The football team debuted one year later.

SETTING THE FOUNDATION

The University of Miami opened its doors in 1925 in Coral Gables, Florida. The Hurricanes played their first football game one year later, on October 30, 1926. That was 57 years after the first college football game.

The Hurricanes began with a 7–0 defeat over Rollins College. Despite only fielding a freshman team in 1926, Miami went 8–0. That set a strong foundation for the program's future.

Howard "Cub" Buck led the Hurricanes in their early years. Buck had been a standout lineman for the NFL's Green Bay Packers during the early 1920s. He coached the Hurricanes for three years, from 1926 to 1928. In 1927, Miami fielded its first varsity team. The Hurricanes started 2–0 that season, but they finished just 3–6–1.

Despite Miami's strong first season, it took a while for the Hurricanes to consistently win on the varsity level.

THE ORANGE BOWL

Burdine Stadium was built in 1937. It was later renamed Orange Bowl Stadium because of the prestigious Orange Bowl game played there at the end of each college football season. For 70 years, the Orange Bowl was one of the great football stadiums in the United States. It was home to the Miami Hurricanes football team for seven decades. It also was the home of the NFL's Miami Dolphins from 1966 to 1986. The Orange Bowl game was played in the stadium every year from 1938 to 1995, and then again in 1999. The stadium also was host to five of the first 13 Super Bowls.

In 1987, the Dolphins moved into the brand-new Sun Life Stadium (then Joe Robbie Stadium). About 10 years later, the Orange Bowl game moved there as well. Finally, in 2008, the Hurricanes also moved to Sun Life Stadium. The Orange Bowl was demolished that year. Major League Baseball's Marlins Park now stands in its place.

It also took a while to find a coach who would stick around. Five different men coached the Hurricanes from 1926 to 1936. Under Tom McCann, the Hurricanes went to the Palm Festival after the 1932 and 1933 seasons. The Palm Festival became the Orange Bowl after the 1934 season. McCann's Hurricanes played in the first official Orange Bowl but lost 26–0 to Bucknell.

Irl Tubbs took over as coach after that. He had some success during his two seasons at the helm. He led the Hurricanes to a 5–3 record in 1935. Then in 1936, he led them to a 6–2–2 mark. That set a school record for wins at the varsity level. After that season, however, Tubbs left to coach at Iowa.

Miami found the first of its several great coaches after that. Jack Harding took over as the Hurricanes' coach in 1937. Before that, he had been a successful coach at Scranton University in Pennsylvania for more than 10 years. He made an instant impact at Miami.

HURRICANES

The Hurricanes beat Georgia Southern 40–0 in Harding's first game in charge, on October 1, 1937. That season also was significant for another reason. It was the first season the Hurricanes played at the Orange Bowl, originally called Burdine Stadium. The Orange Bowl was home to Hurricanes football games from 1937 to 2007.

Harding coached Miami from 1937 to 1942, and again from 1945 to 1947. He missed two seasons while serving in the US Navy during World War II. Former Miami player Eddie Dunn, considered one of the first Hurricanes stars, coached the team while Harding was away.

Harding led the Hurricanes to a 54–32–3 record during his nine seasons. That included a 9–1–1 record in 1945. His teams won at least seven games in five seasons. Perhaps the biggest game of Harding's time came on January 1, 1946. That day the Hurricanes defeated Holy Cross 13–6 in the Orange Bowl. The win also was Miami's 100th in football.

Harding left a lasting legacy at Miami. He resigned as coach in 1947 and became the school's athletic director. He remained in that position until his death in 1963. It was Harding who helped Miami become nationally known as a football team. He put together the football schedule and made sure the Hurricanes were tested against strong opponents. Miami routinely went up against national powers such as Notre Dame, Michigan State, and Alabama.

The school turned to former Virginia Tech coach Andy Gustafson to fill Harding's role as football coach. He picked up right where Harding left off and guided Miami for 16 largely successful seasons.

SETTING THE FOUNDATION

Gustafson's teams went 93–65–3. Through 2011, nobody had coached the Hurricanes longer. No coach had won more games at Miami, either. During Gustafson's 16 seasons, Miami had a winning record 11 times and played in four bowl games. Gustafson also played a big role in helping Miami gain national attention. While Harding scheduled tough games, Gustafson's teams often won those tough games. His Hurricanes reached the top 20 in the AP rankings in nine different seasons. The AP Poll is one of the most respected in college football. Following the 1963 season, Gustafson retired from coaching and became Miami's athletic director, again following in Harding's footsteps.

In addition to coaching the Hurricanes, Harding and Gustafson had two other things in common. Both were Hall of Fame players at the University of Pittsburgh.

Having back-to-back Hall of Fame coaches spoiled the Hurricanes and their fans. After Gustafson left, Miami went through 15 years of

THE MATADOR

Some Miami fans would argue that George Mira Sr., nicknamed "The Matador," was the greatest Hurricane of them all. Mira quarterbacked the team during the early 1960s. He set most of the school's passing records, some of which still stood in 2011. In 1961, Mira took Miami to the Liberty Bowl. In 1962, he took them to the Gotham Bowl. His No. 10 jersey has been retired by the school, and he was inducted into the school's Sports Hall of Fame in 1973. His son, George Mira Jr., joined him in the school's Hall of Fame in 2002. George Mira Jr., was a standout linebacker at Miami from 1984 to 1987.

Miami defenders chase down Clemson tailback Billy Hair during the Gator Bowl following the 1951 season.

mediocrity, from 1964 to 1978. During those seasons, Miami's record was 70–87–3, and it had six different head coaches. Charlie Tate, who followed Gustafson, led the Hurricanes to back-to-back bowl games in 1966 and 1967. But those were the only two bowl games Miami played in during those 15 years.

At the end of the 1978 season, Miami's program was firmly established. The Hurricanes had been playing football for more than 50 years. They had yet to reach college football's peak, but that was about to change.

Miami quarterback Jim Kelly scrambles away from Texas defenders during a 1981 game.

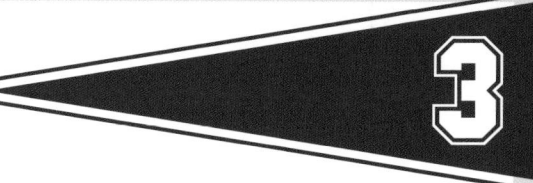

HURRICANES REACH THE TOP

WHEN HOWARD SCHNELLENBERGER WAS HIRED TO COACH MIAMI IN 1979, THE HURRICANES WERE A MESS. THE PROGRAM HAD LOST ITS WINNING FORMULA. FANS DID NOT CARE MUCH ABOUT THE TEAM, EITHER. AN AVERAGE OF JUST 17,236 FANS WENT TO GAMES IN 1976. THAT WAS A SIGNIFICANT DROP FROM THE NEARLY 50,000 FANS THAT WENT TO GAMES DURING THE 1960s.

Schnellenberger had been a longtime offensive coordinator for the NFL's Miami Dolphins. The Hurricanes went just 5–6 in his first season, in 1979. However, freshman quarterback Jim Kelly led Miami to a 26–10 upset at nineteenth-ranked Penn State that season. The win signaled that the team was improving.

The 1980 Hurricanes went 9–3 and beat Virginia Tech in the Peach Bowl. It was Miami's first bowl game since 1967. In 1981, the Hurricanes went 9–2. That included a 17–14 win over top-ranked Penn State. However, Miami was barred

QUARTERBACK U

During the 1980s and into the 1990s, Miami was known as "Quarterback U." Seven of the quarterbacks who guided Miami from 1980 to 2002 later played in the NFL. Perhaps the most successful was Jim Kelly, who was Miami's starting quarterback from 1980 to 1982 and was later selected to the Pro Football Hall of Fame.

Among the other star quarterbacks for Miami who later went to the NFL were Bernie Kosar (Miami's starter from 1983 to 1984), Vinny Testaverde (1985 to 1986), Steve Walsh (1987 to 1988), Craig Erickson (1989 to 1990), Gino Torretta (1991 to 1992), and Ken Dorsey (2000 to 2002). Kosar led Miami to its first national title as a freshman in 1983. Testaverde became Miami's first Heisman Trophy winner in 1986 and the first Hurricanes player to be selected first in the NFL Draft. And Torretta led the Hurricanes to their first perfect season in 1991.

from bowl games that year. The National Collegiate Athletic Association (NCAA) had put Miami on probation for recruiting violations.

Hopes were sky-high going into 1982. Kelly was a Heisman Trophy candidate. Schnellenberger believed his team could win a national title. "Go for it," was his motto for the year. "They have a chance to be a very good football team," he said. However, Kelly injured his shoulder in the third game and did not play the rest of the year. The team finished a disappointing 7–4.

Kelly was gone in 1983, but the Hurricanes were well on their way to greatness. Freshman quarterback Bernie Kosar stepped in and quickly starred. Miami lost to rival Florida to start the year. But Kosar then led the Hurricanes to 10 consecutive wins. That gave the team the number-five ranking going into the Orange Bowl game.

Miami faced top-ranked Nebraska in the Orange Bowl on January 2, 1984.

Hurricanes wide receiver Stanley Shakespeare leaps for a catch during the 1984 Orange Bowl against Nebraska.

At the time, the two top-ranked teams were not guaranteed to meet in a bowl game. Most fans expected Nebraska to easily win. After all, the Cornhuskers had won 22 straight games. But the Hurricanes were ready.

Miami's defense smothered Nebraska's high-powered offense for three quarters. Kosar, meanwhile, guided the offense into the fourth quarter with a stunning 31–17 lead. Nebraska did not go away, though. It scored a touchdown to pull within seven points. Then the Cornhuskers again scored with 48 seconds to play, cutting Miami's lead to one. The score was 31–30. All that was left to tie the score was the extra point attempt. Nebraska could have kicked the extra point—a tie likely would have given it the national title. But instead, the Cornhuskers tried a

HURRICANES REACH THE TOP

two-point conversion for the win. A pass attempt fell incomplete, though, and Miami was victorious.

As it turned out, three of the four teams ranked ahead of Miami lost their bowl games. And in the final vote, the Hurricanes jumped all four to number one. For the first time, the Hurricanes were the champions of college football. "No words can describe it," Schnellenberger said.

Schnellenberger had transformed the program in just five short years. The Hurricanes were winners on the field. And fans again were showing up in large numbers. There were 72,549 people at the Orange Bowl win against Nebraska. But Schnellenberger did not stay to defend his title. He left to take a job in the upstart United States Football League, a rival league to the NFL. However, the team never materialized and Schnellenberger was out of work.

The Hurricanes continued to win, though. Schnellenberger had stocked the roster with talented players. New coach Jimmy Johnson picked up where Schnellenberger left off.

BLADES EXCELS

Bennie Blades was one of the best defensive players to ever wear a Miami uniform. The safety played for the Hurricanes from 1984 to 1987, helping them win a national title in his senior season. Blades led the nation with 10 interceptions in 1986. In 1987, he won the Jim Thorpe Award. It is given each year to the best defensive back in the country. Blades, who went on to play nine years in the NFL, was inducted into the College Football Hall of Fame in 2006.

Miami quarterback Vinny Testaverde led Miami to the Fiesta Bowl following the 1986 season.

In 1984, Johnson and the Hurricanes began the season with wins over top-ranked Auburn and seventeenth-ranked Florida. That vaulted them to number one in the country. However, Miami ended up finishing 8–4 that season. It would be Johnson's worst season in Coral Gables.

Miami finished the 1985 regular season at 10–1 and ranked second. The Hurricanes would have been crowned national champions with a Sugar Bowl win over eighth-ranked Tennessee. But Tennessee dominated, winning 35–7.

In 1986, Johnson led the Hurricanes to an 11–0 regular-season record. Heisman Trophy-winning quarterback Vinny Testaverde was the star for Miami. Top-ranked Miami battled second-ranked Penn State in

HURRICANES

the Fiesta Bowl on January 2, 1987. The winner would be the national champion. The Hurricanes were confident—almost cocky—going into the game against Penn State. However, Testaverde had the worst day of his college career. The Hurricanes never got rolling. Testaverde threw five interceptions in the game, including one near the goal line in the final seconds of the game. Penn State won 14–10.

Johnson and the Hurricanes finally broke through in 1987. Nebraska and Oklahoma spent almost the entire season ranked in the top two, with Miami at number three. Oklahoma's win over Nebraska opened the door for Miami. The second-ranked Hurricanes and the top-ranked Oklahoma Sooners squared off in the Orange Bowl on January 1, 1988. Miami went into the game at 11–0.

Miami sophomore quarterback Steve Walsh had a great game against Oklahoma. On defense, sophomore linebacker Bernard Clark was sensational. And as a team, the Hurricanes proved their greatness with a 20–14 win. That gave Miami its second national title.

Miami nearly won another national title in 1988. After a 23–3 win over Nebraska in the Orange Bowl, Miami finished the season with

AT THE TOP

Miami had a remarkable run of success from 1983 to 1994. The Hurricanes found themselves ranked number one in the country at some point during nine of those 12 years. Miami reached the top ranking during seven straight seasons, from 1986 to 1992. In those seven seasons, the Hurricanes never finished a year outside of the top three.

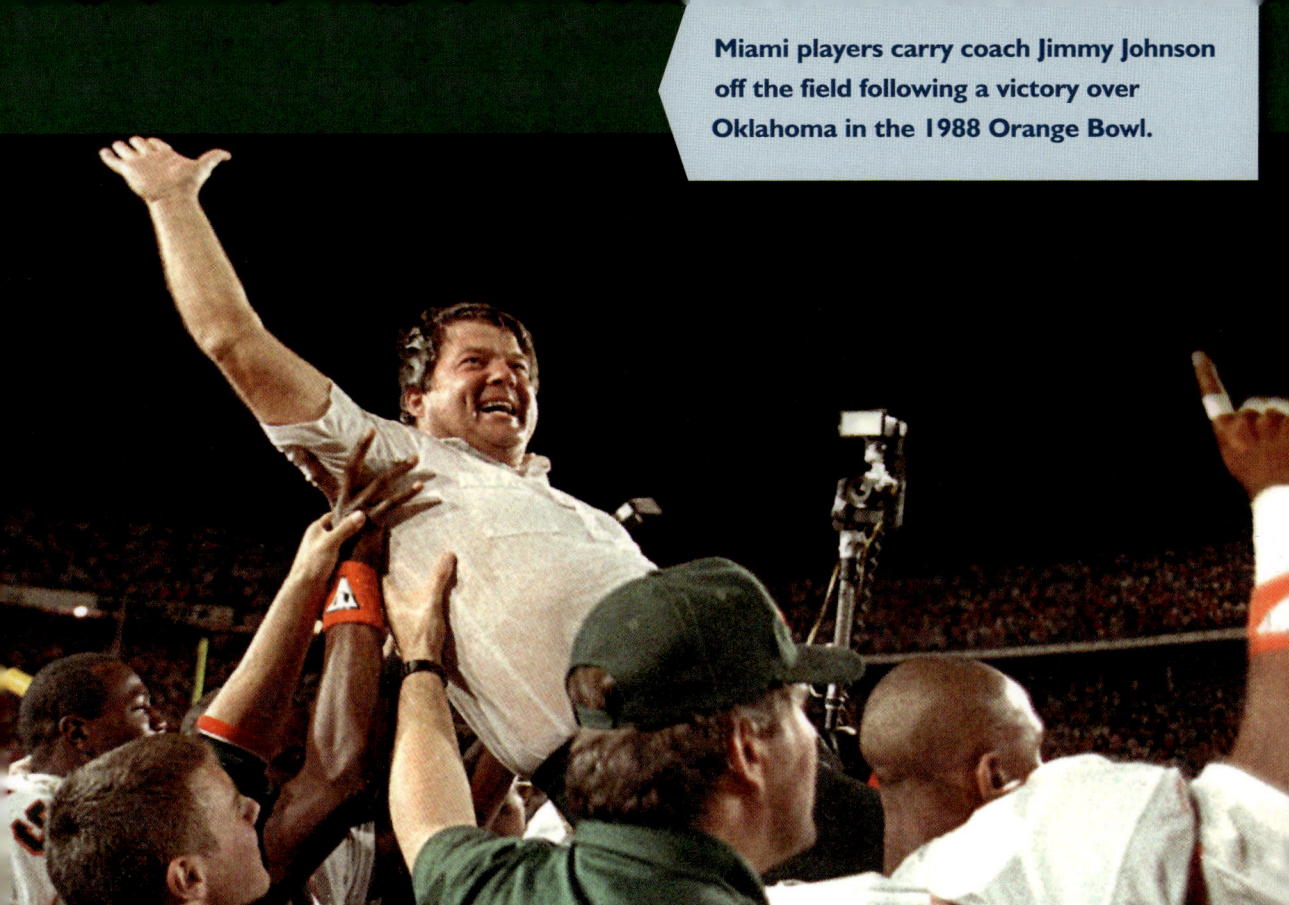

Miami players carry coach Jimmy Johnson off the field following a victory over Oklahoma in the 1988 Orange Bowl.

an 11–1 record. The only blemish was a 31–30 loss at Notre Dame. Miami finished the year ranked number two. Notre Dame won the championship.

Johnson left Miami after the 1988 season to coach the NFL's Dallas Cowboys, and later, the Miami Dolphins. It was with the Hurricanes, however, that Johnson became a household name.

"My time at the University of Miami really defines my career," Johnson said. "It was probably the most fun time I ever had in my life prior to now, and we were able to do some things that I was extremely proud of."

Miami tight end Rob Chudzinski grabs a touchdown pass against Alabama during the 1990 Sugar Bowl.

TRADITION CONTINUES

WITH JIMMY JOHNSON GONE TO THE DALLAS COWBOYS, THE HURRICANES WERE ONCE AGAIN IN SEARCH OF A NEW COACH. THEY FOUND ONE ACROSS THE COUNTRY IN WASHINGTON.

Dennis Erickson had led Washington State to a 9–3 record in 1988. That included a victory in the Aloha Bowl. Going to Miami was a major step up for Erickson, who had been coaching for 20 years. At Washington State, a 9–3 record was a great season. Miami, however, was beginning to expect championships. The school had recently won the 1983 and 1987 national titles.

Erickson quickly proved he was up to the task. In fact, his six years at Miami could be considered the best of any coach in school history. From 1989 to 1994, he led the Hurricanes to a remarkable 63–9 record. As of 2012, he was also the only coach in Miami history to win two national titles.

HURRICANES

Erickson won his first championship in his first season, 1989. A mid-season loss at Florida State was the only blemish as Miami went 11–1. That season was capped by a 33–25 win over Alabama in the Sugar Bowl. Much like previous Miami teams, the 1989 squad was loaded with talent. Craig Erickson—no relation to the coach—was the starting quarterback and played well. He was injured and missed the game against Florida State, however.

The defense is what really shined. It gave up just 10.6 points per game. One of Miami's most impressive performances came late in November with a 27–10 win over top-ranked Notre Dame. Before that loss, Notre Dame had won 23 games in a row. Miami's defense had eight players who were drafted into the NFL the next spring. One of the team's best players was defensive tackle Cortez Kennedy. He was taken with the third pick in the draft. Kennedy was an All-American for Miami. And he went on to become a Pro Football Hall of Famer.

Two years later, the Hurricanes were back on top. Led by junior quarterback Gino Torretta and an awesome defense, Miami rolled to

A NEW ERA

Prior to 1991, Miami had always been an independent team. That meant the Hurricanes did not belong to any conference. But that changed in 1991. That year, Miami became a charter member for football in the Big East Conference. Boston College, Pittsburgh, Rutgers, Syracuse, Temple, Virginia Tech, and West Virginia were the other members. Miami won at least a share of nine Big East titles from 1991 to 2003.

Miami quarterback Gino Torretta poses with his receiving corps prior to the 1992 season.

an 8–0 start. During those eight games, the Hurricanes outscored their opponents 289–58. All but one of the wins came by 24 points or more.

Miami visited top-ranked Florida State for its ninth game that season. The Seminoles had become a bitter rival of Miami's. This game was one of the most memorable in the rivalry. Miami rallied in the fourth quarter to take a 17–16 lead. Then Florida State marched down the field. The Seminoles nearly won the game with a field goal. But the kick sailed wide right and Miami got the win. The game has become known as "Wide Right I." That was actually the first of five games in a 12-year span in which Florida State missed a late field goal in a loss to Miami. Four of the missed field goals went wide right of the goal post.

TRADITION CONTINUES

Miami won its final two games to complete a perfect regular season. Then the Hurricanes dominated Nebraska 22–0 in the Orange Bowl to win their fourth national championship. This one, however, was a split national title. Washington also went 12–0. It was voted number one in the Coaches' Poll and other major polls.

The 1992 Hurricanes completed another perfect regular season at 11–0. That gave them 29 consecutive victories. They took that win streak and the number-one ranking into the Sugar Bowl against second-ranked Alabama on January 1, 1993. The winner would be crowned the national champion. Although Torretta was the Heisman Trophy winner, Miami's offense never got anything going. The Hurricanes never scored an offensive touchdown in the 34–13 loss.

Miami remained in national-title contention for the next two years. Erickson left after the 1994 season to coach in the NFL. As good as Erickson's teams were, however, he left under a dark cloud. The NCAA found that Miami had violated several rules under Erickson. Miami was put on probation. That meant the team could not play in a bowl game in 1995. The program also had more than 30 scholarships taken away.

THE WIN STREAK

Few teams got out of Orange Bowl Stadium with a win during the 1980s and 1990s. In 1994, the Hurricanes opened the season with a 56–0 win over Georgia Southern. That gave them 58 straight wins in the Orange Bowl—a streak that began in 1985. Washington put a stop to that streak in Miami's next home game, however, winning 38–20.

> Miami's Warren Sapp (76) celebrates after a sack in the 1995 Orange Bowl as Dwayne Johnson (94) looks on.

Still, 14 different players earned first-team All-America honors during Erickson's years. Kicker Carlos Huerta was one of them. He kicked an NCAA-record 157 straight extra points and remained one of the all-time leading scorers in NCAA history through 2011.

Future NFL stars Russell Maryland and Warren Sapp dominated on the defensive line during the early 1990s. Maurice Crum, Darrin Smith, and Michael Barrow were three of the best linebackers Miami has ever had. Darryl Williams and Ryan McNeil were top-flight defensive backs who had long NFL careers.

As Erickson and those star players moved on, so did Miami. A new coach was on his way, but the expectations would remain the same.

TRADITION CONTINUES

Miami's punishing defense stops Florida tailback Earnest Graham in his tracks at the 2001 Sugar Bowl.

SEEKING A RETURN TO THE TOP

WITH MIAMI GOING THROUGH OFF-THE-FIELD TROUBLES, BUTCH DAVIS RETURNED TO CORAL GABLES TO COACH THE HURRICANES. HE HAD BEEN AN ASSISTANT UNDER COACH JIMMY JOHNSON. DAVIS HAD THEN FOLLOWED JOHNSON TO THE DALLAS COWBOYS. AFTER RETURNING TO MIAMI, DAVIS LED THE HURRICANES FROM 1995 TO 2000. AND HE DID A GREAT JOB. HIS TEAMS WENT 51–20, INCLUDING A 4–0 RECORD IN BOWL GAMES.

Davis's teams never played for a national title, but many believe his 2000 squad should have. That team went 10–1 during the regular season. Its only loss came against Washington in the second game of the year. In the fifth game, Miami defeated top-ranked Florida State. At the end of the regular season, Oklahoma was ranked number one and Miami was number two. However, the BCS system had begun after the 1998 season. It determined that third-ranked Florida State should go to the national championship game instead of Miami. Hurricanes fans are still upset about that.

Miami instead went to the Sugar Bowl and rolled past rival Florida 37–20. That was Davis's last game at Miami. He left for the NFL's Cleveland Browns. Davis was the fourth consecutive Miami head coach to leave the program for a job in professional football.

Popular assistant Larry Coker replaced Davis. Many players were in favor of having Coker take over. At the time, Coker was 53 years old and had spent more than 20 years as an assistant coach. Despite never being a head coach, Miami took a chance on him.

From 2001 to 2006, Coker guided the Hurricanes to a 60–15 record. He led them to a national title in 2001. He started his tenure 24–0 before losing the 2002 national title game. After a rough 6–6 regular season in 2006, Coker was fired. Still, through 2011, his 60 wins ranked third all-time among Miami coaches.

Coker took the Hurricanes to six bowl games in his six years, winning four of them. Johnson, Dennis Erickson, and Coker are the only Miami coaches to go to bowl games in every season on the job.

LEWIS INTIMIDATES

Those who follow the NFL know that Ray Lewis is one of the best linebackers in professional football history. He is one of the best in college football history, too. Lewis starred at Miami from 1993 to 1995. He developed a reputation for being a punishing hitter. Lewis was a first-round pick of the NFL's Baltimore Ravens in 1996. In 2011, he finished his sixteenth season as a Raven and was still going strong. He was a 13-time Pro Bowl player and was the NFL Defensive Player of the Year in 2000 and 2003.

Miami running back Willis McGahee runs for a touchdown during the 2003 Fiesta Bowl against Ohio State.

By 2006, however, Miami had fallen on hard times. Coker and the Hurricanes prided themselves on their cleaned-up image early in his tenure. But several on-the-field altercations with opponents tarnished that image in 2006. It did not help Coker that the Hurricanes had lost their winning edge.

That season, Miami lost two of its first three games. A four-game losing streak in the middle of the season dropped the team to 5–6. The Hurricanes needed a 17–14 win against Boston College in the final game to finish 6–6 and earn a trip to a bowl game. Teams must win six games in order to be selected to a bowl game. Prior to the bowl game, Miami announced that Coker would be fired. However, he still coached the MPC Computers Bowl, defeating Nevada 21–20.

The 2006 season was a rare year in which the Hurricanes did not finish in the AP Top 25 rankings. From 1980 to 2006, Miami failed to finish in the rankings just three times—1982, 1997, and 2006. The coaching change did not bring the success the school had hoped for. During the first five seasons after Coker's firing, from 2007 to 2011, Miami had a combined record of just 34–29.

To replace Coker, Miami hired Randy Shannon. He had been a starting linebacker on Miami's 1987 national championship team. He then spent seven years as a Miami assistant coach, from 1991 to 1997. Then he worked on the staff of the NFL's Miami Dolphins for three years. Shannon returned to the Hurricanes in 2001 and worked as Coker's defensive coordinator for six years.

A NEW HOME

After 13 years in the Big East Conference, Miami made a big decision in 2003. The Hurricanes decided to leave the Big East and join the Atlantic Coast Conference (ACC). Miami began playing in the ACC in 2004 and has been a part of that conference ever since. After dominating the Big East, Miami has not found the same success in the ACC. The conference is divided into two divisions, with the division winners squaring off each year in a championship game. Through 2011, Miami had yet to win its division, let alone a championship game.

Miami coach Larry Coker and his players run onto the field before a 2006 game against Boston College.

Shannon's team began the 2007 season with a 4–1 record, but it lost six of its last seven games. With a 5–7 record, Miami missed out on a bowl game for the first time since 1997. The Hurricanes only improved slightly to 7–6 the next season.

In 2009, the Hurricanes jumped back into the national spotlight. After a 5–1 start, they moved up to number eight in the country. Led by sophomore quarterback Jacory Harris, Miami had its best season in several years. Harris threw for 3,352 yards and 24 touchdowns.

HURRICANES

The Hurricanes went 9–4 and finished the season ranked number 19. Fans were once again excited about the future of Miami football.

More disappointment came in 2010, though. After the great 2009 season, Miami felt it had a championship-caliber team in 2010. The Hurricanes began the year ranked number 13. But they again finished the season unranked. They went 7–5 during the regular season.

Shannon did a good job of cleaning up the program off the field. On the field, however, he was just 28–22. The school fired him after the 2010 regular season.

Al Golden was hired as Shannon's replacement before the 2011 season. Golden had turned around a struggling program at Temple. And Miami hoped he could do the same for the Hurricanes.

Golden's first season ended with a 6–6 record. There were plenty of bright spots, though. Harris threw for 2,486 yards and 20 touchdowns. Sophomore running back Lamar Miller rushed for 1,272 yards. The Hurricanes also picked up a pair of wins over number 17 Ohio State and number 20 Georgia Tech.

SCANDAL AT MIAMI

In 2011, Miami booster Nevin Shapiro detailed how he gave improper financial benefits to at least 72 players from 2002 to 2010. After an NCAA investigation, several Miami players were suspended for part of the 2011 season. That included starting quarterback Jacory Harris, who missed the first game of the season.

Miami quarterback Jacory Harris surveys the field before taking the snap during a 2011 game against Boston College.

To many Miami fans, the days of national dominance seemed long ago. Yet the Hurricanes were hopeful that they would once again become an elite team.

"Al has done a fantastic job of rebuilding and solidifying the foundation of our football program while fostering success both on and off the field," athletic director Shawn Eichorst said at the end of the 2011 season. "He has been a first-class representative of our university and I am confident that with Al leading the way, our future is very bright."

SEEKING A RETURN TO THE TOP

TIMELINE

1926 — Miami plays its first football game on October 30, defeating Rollins College 7–0.

1927 — The Hurricanes play their first varsity football game, defeating Rollins 39–3 on October 29.

1933 — On January 1, the Hurricanes play in their first bowl game—the Palm Festival bowl in Miami. They defeat Manhattan College 7–0.

1937 — Burdine Stadium opens, and Miami begins playing its home games there. The stadium was later renamed the Orange Bowl.

1950 — After a 9–1–1 record, Miami is ranked number 15 in the AP Poll. It is the first time Miami finishes a season in the AP rankings.

1987 — Jimmy Johnson, who replaced Schnellenberger as coach, leads the Hurricanes to their second national title and their first undefeated season at 12–0.

1989 — In his first season as coach, Dennis Erickson leads Miami to its second national title in three years. The Hurricanes go 11–1 and win the Sugar Bowl on January 1, 1990.

1991 — Miami is a charter football member of the Big East Conference. For the third time in five years, Miami finishes as the national champion after going 12–0.

1992 — Quarterback Gino Torretta becomes the second Miami player to win the Heisman Trophy.

1994 — Miami sees its 58-game home winning streak come to a close. It was still the longest home win streak in school history through 2011.

1963 — Andy Gustafson, the winningest coach in Miami history, retires from coaching. In 16 seasons, Gustafson led the Hurricanes to a 93–65–3 record.

1966 — Led by coach Charlie Tate, the Hurricanes finish 8–2–1 and earn their second postseason top-10 ranking, at number nine. They cap the season with a win against Virginia Tech in the Liberty Bowl.

1979 — Howard Schnellenberger, an assistant coach with the Miami Dolphins of the NFL, is hired as the Hurricanes' head coach.

1983 — Schnellenberger and quarterback Bernie Kosar lead the Hurricanes to their first national title with an 11–1 record. After turning around the program in just five years, Schnellenberger resigns for a job in professional football.

1986 — Quarterback Vinny Testaverde becomes the first Miami player to win the Heisman Trophy.

2000 — The Hurricanes finish the season ranked number two after a controversial decision keeps them out of the BCS national championship game.

2001 — First-year head coach Larry Coker leads Miami to its fifth national championship. The Hurricanes go 12–0 and dominate Nebraska in the Rose Bowl on January 3, 2002.

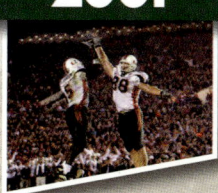

2003 — Going for a second straight national title, Miami takes a 34-game win streak into the Fiesta Bowl on January 3 but loses in double-overtime to Ohio State.

2003 — The Hurricanes finish 11–2 and ranked number five. It is Miami's twelfth top-five finish since 1983.

2011 — Al Golden is hired as the new head coach of the Hurricanes.

QUICK STATS

PROGRAM INFO
University of Miami Hurricanes (1926–)

NATIONAL CHAMPIONSHIPS
(* DENOTES SHARED TITLE)
1983, 1987, 1989, 1991*, 2001

OTHER ACHIEVEMENTS
BCS bowl appearances (1999–): 4
Big East championships (1991–2003): 9
ACC championships (2004–): 0
Bowl record: 18–15

HEISMAN TROPHY WINNERS
Vinny Testaverde, 1986
Gino Torretta, 1992

KEY PLAYERS
(POSITION[S]; SEASONS WITH TEAM)
Bennie Blades (DB; 1985–87)
Don Bosseler (FB; 1953–56)
Jim Dooley (HB; 1949–51)
Eddie Dunn (RB; 1936–38)
Ted Hendricks (DE; 1966–68)
Michael Irvin (WR; 1985–87)
Jim Kelly (QB; 1979–82)
Cortez Kennedy (DT; 1988–89)
Bernie Kosar (QB; 1983–84)
Ray Lewis (LB; 1993–95)
Russell Maryland (DT; 1986–90)
George Mira (QB; 1961–63)
Dan Morgan (LB; 1997–2000)
Jim Otto (C; 1957–59)
Vinny Testaverde (QB; 1982, 1984–86)
Gino Torretta (QB; 1989–92)

KEY COACHES
Larry Coker (2001–06):
    60–15; 4–2 (bowl games)
Dennis Erickson (1989–94):
    63–9; 3–3 (bowl games)
Jimmy Johnson (1984–88):
    52–9; 2–3 (bowl games)

HOME STADIUM
Sun Life Stadium (2008–)

* All statistics through 2011 season

QUOTES & ANECDOTES

Miami and Florida State have faced each other nearly every year since 1951. The intensity of the rivalry was cranked up in the 1980s, 1990s, and early 2000s. That was mainly because one of the teams—if not both—was in national title contention every year. From 1983 to 2005, they played 24 consecutive games in which at least one of them was ranked in the top 10. In 19 of those games, at least one of them was ranked in the top five. And in 13 of those games, both were ranked in the top 10. Seven times, one of them was ranked number one.

While Miami experienced a lot of success on the football field during the 1980s and 1990s, it also went through a lot of troubles off the field. The program had recruiting violations and academic issues with its players. It was accused of giving improper benefits to its players. Several players also had run-ins with the law. Problems were so bad that in the June 12, 1995, issue of *Sports Illustrated*, the magazine urged Miami to drop its football program.

"When you get insulted at the beginning of the week, like I was insulted about my trophy, that kind of insulted the whole team." —Miami star defensive tackle Russell Maryland, after Texas offensive lineman Stan Thomas said Maryland, the Outland Trophy winner, was just "a good player." The Hurricanes went on to dominate Texas 46–3 in the 1991 Cotton Bowl in a game infamous for the Hurricanes' excessive taunting and celebrations.

GLOSSARY

All-American
A player chosen as one of the best amateurs in the country in a particular activity.

conference
In sports, a group of teams that plays each other each season.

consensus
Unanimous agreement.

draft
A system used by professional sports leagues to select new players in order to spread incoming talent among all teams. The NFL Draft is held each spring.

inducted
To be included as a member of a hall of fame.

probation
For college athletics, it is a period of time where the NCAA will keep a close eye on a team that has broken the rules.

recruiting
Trying to entice a player to come to a certain school.

retired
Officially ended one's career. If a team retired a jersey number, no future player is allowed to wear it for that team.

rival
An opponent that brings out great emotion in a team, its fans, and its players.

scholarships
Financial assistance awarded to students to help them pay for school. Top athletes earn scholarships to represent a college through its sports teams.

upset
A result where the supposedly worse team defeats the supposedly better team.

varsity
The main team that represents a school.

FOR MORE INFORMATION

FURTHER READING

Feldman, Bruce. *The University of Miami Football Vault.* Florence, AL: Whitman Publishing, 2009.

Martz, Jim. *Tales from the Miami Hurricanes Sideline.* Champaign, IL: Sports Publishing, 2004.

Hurricaneology Trivia Challenge. Lewis Center, OH: Kick The Ball, 2008.

WEB LINKS

To learn more about the Miami Hurricanes, visit ABDO Publishing Company online at **www.abdopublishing.com**. Web sites about the Hurricanes are featured on our Book Links page. These links are routinely monitored and updated to provide the most current information available.

PLACES TO VISIT

College Football Hall of Fame
111 South St. Joseph St.
South Bend, IN 46601
1-800-440-FAME (3263)
www.collegefootball.org

This hall of fame and museum highlights the greatest players and moments in the history of college football. Among the former Hurricanes enshrined here are Bennie Blades, Russell Maryland, and Ted Hendricks, along with former coaches Andy Gustafson, Jack Harding, and Jimmy Johnson.

Sun Life Stadium
347 Don Shula Drive
Miami Gardens, FL 33056
305-623-6100
www.sunlifestadium.com

This has been Miami's home field since 2008. The Hurricanes share the field with the NFL's Miami Dolphins.

INDEX

Barrow, Michael, 33
Bibla, Martin, 8
Blades, Bennie, 24
Bowl Championship Series (BCS), 6, 7, 35
Buchanon, Phillip, 8
Buck, Howard "Cub," 15
Burdine Stadium. See Orange Bowl Stadium
Coker, Larry (coach), 7–8, 9, 36, 37-38
Crum, Maurice, 33
Davis, Butch (coach), 7, 35, 36
Dorsey, Ken, 5, 6, 8, 10–11, 13, 22
Dunn, Eddie (coach), 17
Eichorst, Shawn (athletic director), 41
Erickson, Craig, 22, 30
Erickson, Dennis (coach), 29-30, 32, 33, 36
Fiesta Bowl, 13, 25–26

Golden, Al (coach), 40, 41
Gonzalez, Joaquin, 8
Gustafson, Andy (coach), 17–19
Harding, Jack, 16–17, 18
Harris, Jacory, 39, 40
Huerta, Carlos, 33
Johnson, Andre, 5, 8, 13
Johnson, Jimmy (coach), 24–25, 26, 27, 29, 35, 36
Joseph, William, 8–9
Kelly, Jim, 21, 22
Kennedy, Cortez, 30
Kosar, Bernie, 22, 23
Maryland, Russell, 33
McCann, Tom (coach), 16
McDougle, Jerome, 8–9
McKinnie, Bryant, 8, 13
McNeil, Ryan, 33
Mira, George, Sr., 18
Morgan, Dan, 13
Orange Bowl, 6–7, 16, 17, 22–23, 24, 26, 32
Orange Bowl (stadium), 16, 17, 32

Portis, Clinton, 5, 8, 11
Reed, Ed, 8, 10, 11-12
Romberg, Brett, 8, 13
Rose Bowl, 5, 11
Rumph, Mike, 8, 10
Sapp, Warren, 33
Schnellenberger, Howard (coach), 21, 22, 24
Shannon, Randy (coach), 38–39, 40
Shockey, Jeremy, 8, 10–11
Sievers, Todd, 8
Smith, Darrin, 33
Sugar Bowl, 7, 25, 30, 32, 36
Tate, Charlie, 19
Taylor, Sean, 9
Testaverde, Vinny, 22, 25, 26
Torretta, Gino, 22, 30–31, 32
Tubbs, Irl (coach), 16
Vilma, Jonathan, 9, 10
Walsh, Steve, 22, 26
Walters, Matt, 10
Williams, D. J., 9
Williams, Darryl, 33

ABOUT THE AUTHOR

Brian Howell is a freelance writer based in Denver, Colorado. He has been a sports journalist for nearly 20 years, writing about high school, college, and professional athletics. In addition, he has written books about sports and history. A native of Colorado, he lives with his wife and four children in his home state.